SURFING

with the

GREAT WHITE

SHARK

A true story about one of the worst recorded shark attacks on a surfer in history!

SURFING

with the

GREAT WHITE

SHARK

**by survivor
Kenny Doudt**

Shark Bite Publishing   **Lihue, Hawaii**

Cover Painting by: Allan Gibbons; Photo of Kenny Doudt by: Sam Foster; Photo of Great White Crusing Courtesy of Howard Hall of Howard Hall Productions

Cover Design: Kenny Doudt & Dale Schroeder

Publisher's Cataloging in Publication
(Prepared by Quality Books Inc.)

Doudt, Kenny R., 1953-
    Surfing with the great white shark/by survivor Kenny Doudt.
    p. cm.
    Includes bibliographical references.
    ISBN 0-9633342-7-1
    1. Doudt, Kenny R. 2. Shark attacks—Oregon. 3. White shark.
    4. Surfing—Oregon. I. Title.

QL638.93.D68 1992   597.31'09795
                                            QBI92-1675
    Library of Congress Catalog Card Number: 92-090967

To my sons...
Jeremy and Justin.

Introduction

The following is the story of an experience I had when I was 26 years old. It occurred while I was surfing on a cold winter day in Oregon in 1979. Though it has been many years ago now, the experience was so terrifying that it is still very real to me today. This incident, in which I almost lost my life, involved an encounter with a primitive ruthless creature who stalks the ocean depths......*A Great White Shark.*

—Kenny Doudt

Acknowledgements

My special thanks to: Bill Blanchard for helping me get my thoughts on paper; Heather Kibby for guiding me in the right direction; Sam Foster for taking the pictures to document my ordeal. I also wish to thank the following people for making the publication of this book possible: National Wildlife Federation, Terry Link, Howard Hall, Leo Dubois, Pollie Oliver, Dr. Spears, Dale Schroeder, Helen Savage, Doug Hewitt, Kauai Community College, Paradise Publishing, Dan Poynter, Publishers Marketing Association, Bonnie Sue Oathes, Leanne Matsuda, Will Welch and everyone who had a good thought about this project.

CONTENTS

CHAPTER I

A FEELING OF TOTAL HELPLESSNESS

I paused midway along the length of the diving board, my attention drawn downward by the sparkling of the sun rays as they danced across the surface of the pool. Looking deeper, the four black tile lines along the bottom were made to look in the rippling water like long, wriggling snakes. Then, I took the three final steps before letting the reaction of the board and the spring in my legs toss me high above the water. I arched gracefully downward, slicing into the pool with barely a splash.

Kicking back to the surface, I shook my head to flick the dripping hair from my eyes. Then I slowly treaded water while I let my mind replay what I considered to be a perfect dive. I felt good, yet something deep in my subconscious bothered me. I noticed a shadow, not my own, moving across the bottom of the pool.

Surfing with the Great White Shark

Kicking harder, I tried to raise myself high enough above the water to get a closer view below the surface. Then I saw it—a light gray shape gliding just off the bottom slowly circling beneath the diving board and accelerating back in my direction.

I kicked backward violently, trying to escape. The shadow rose, getting closer. I rolled over on my stomach and swam as hard as I could. No matter how hard I swam, I barely moved. My arms seemed like leaden weights, my legs moving in slow motion. Each time I looked toward the edge of the pool it seemed farther away. Glancing back over my shoulder, I saw the shadow take shape, a pointed head looming larger, a massive fin breaking the surface. I was lifted by a surge of water as the enormous creature swept past below, raking me with its sandpaper-like skin.

"Oh my God!" I thought. "It's gonna get me." I redoubled my effort to escape, fighting to reach the edge of the pool. Even swimming with all my might, I barely moved. Then the creature circled back. I did not want to look down, but fear drew my head like a magnet and I found the shark's eyes locked with mine in the cold stare of death. Hypnotized, I watched the head emerge from the water, gills flapping, black soulless eyes staring, its gaping mouth revealing rows and rows of razor-sharp teeth as it zeroed in for the kill. I screamed, then sat up.

"Kenny!" a voice said. "You all right? You scared the crap out of me!"

A Feeling of Total Helplessness

Confused, I shook my head and stared around, not knowing where I was, my chest heaving, my heart pounding, sweat pouring off my body. It took me a few seconds to realize I was safe on the beach, a bright sun warming me as it filtered through the fronds on the palm tree swaying high above me. White sand stretched for miles in both directions. A gentle wind riffled the surface of the turquoise sea. In the distance, rugged cliffs rose from the ocean, their tops lined with sugarcane.

"You okay now?" the concerned voice of my buddy asked. "The swell picked up while you were asleep. "Come on. Let's go back out."

"Whew!" I mumbled, a bit calmer. But, my body was still covered with sweat, my pulse racing, traumatic terror still too real. "No thanks. You go on."

My friend, R.T., shook his head as he stared down at me in disbelief.

"Come on, get your board," he said. "Let's go."

"Yeah," I agreed. "Give me a couple of seconds to get my act together."

"Okay bro," R.T. said as he grabbed his board and walked toward the water.

Settling back against the rough trunk of the coconut tree I had been sleeping under, I watched him paddle out through the waves. It worried me that I could not get rid of the dream. It took different forms, various settings—sometimes a pool, sometimes the ocean or a river, but always very intense.

Unable to relax, or get my breathing back to normal, I pushed myself up and walked over the hot sand to my truck and pulled a beer from the ice chest. R.T. was in the lineup, paddling hard to catch a wave. I watched him angle across the face of the wave as it feathered its way toward shore.

"Maybe he's right," I thought. "I should go back out, if for no other reason than to try and shake off that damned dream."

Instead of picking up my board, I popped the top off the cold beer and took a long swallow, annoyed at myself when I found my hands were shaking.

I thought that I could escape the nightmares now that I was in this tropical paradise, but the cold horror still plagued me. It continued to recur with a vengeance, always leaving me shaken and emotionally drained.

I leaned back and took another long swallow of brew and let my mind drift back to the chain of events that had brought on the terrifying nightmare.

CHAPTER II

THE DAY BEFORE

I knew it was going to be another long, cold winter. My job at Breaker's Point, the construction site overlooking one of Oregon's classic breaks, had been a torture to me every day.

Consistent east winds made surfing conditions ideal: the offshore breeze held up wave faces, making clean three to five-foot rights that peeled off one after another with clock-like regularity. The grandstand view all day long from the job site did nothing to improve my state of mind. It was not the work I disliked, but rather the constant torture of watching surfers rip the near perfect waves while I pounded nails into lumber.

I paused after pulling a nail from my nail bag when my eyes were drawn below to a surfer on a bright yellow board, just taking off. He dropped effortlessly down the face of the glassy wave, slicing a deep bottom turn before jamming to the top, then carving a long silver path across the wave's face. The next wave, equally perfect, went by unridden. To see such waste was annoying, angering me into slamming the nail-head deep into the board. I cursed to myself as I again raised the hammer, unable to shake the depression which engulfed my mind.

I was staying with my good friend, Jack, who I called Bird. One cold gray day blended slowly into the next, with very few bright spots in the all-consuming monotony. I had been working at the job site for more than a month, making the same drive to work each morning and then back home in the afternoon. The only noticeable change was that Christmas decorations were beginning to appear in store windows. The sights and sounds of everything depressed me, bringing back mem-

View from jobsite *(Sam Foster)*

ories of past Christmases spent with my two sons, Jeremy 3, and Justin, 2.

It had been just five months since my wife and I had split up. For me, it seemed more like five long years. I felt lost, like life no longer had meaning. The work I once enjoyed and had taken great pride in had become drudgery.

Methodically, without really thinking, I leaned down to grab another two-by-four. A freezing cold rain pelted my back and ran off my rain gear. That day had been the third in a row of working in miserable weather. Although the drizzle continued, it was not heavy enough to block my view of the surf below, where five surfers waited for a wave. Their wetsuits glistened as they sat outside the break, the tips of their boards and their upper bodies plainly visible above the cold, 50-degree water. Anyone who surfed those waters without a full suit wouldn't last more than five minutes.

I remembered how most of the time my hands were so cold after surfing I had a hard time unlocking the car door and turning the ignition key.

But worries about cold water and frigid air disappeared with the anticipated rewards of dropping in on a wave with the surfers I watched from my high vantage point. Winter offshore winds kept the surf ideal. Even though a few locals were out, most waves peeled off unridden. Even as I watched, a big set began to feather off outside and the surfers paddled hard to get over the peak before it broke.

"Darn it!" I muttered, my mood darkening to equal the gloom of the weather. It was all getting to be too much for me to handle. I needed a break—a time to collect my thoughts, to *reevaluate* my life and set a new course. More than anything I just wanted to surf.

Impulsively, I made a decision. I'd quit my job and take the time I needed to sort things out. A few days of good waves would clear my mind. Immediately upon making the decision, I began to feel better.

With my mind made up, I felt like the sun had come out and that the rain had been blown away. Cheerfully humming to myself, I picked up another board and nailed it into place. I decided to finish out the day. I owed the boss that much. But the next day I would be back in the water, surfing with my friends below.

 # CHAPTER III

THE DECISION

Had I noticed a number of significant signs presently affecting the ocean and its ecosystem, I might not have been so anxious to quit my job and get into the water. If I had paid more attention to the weather reports, I'd have known that a major storm system, centered northeast of the Hawaiian Islands, had generated gigantic waves which had pounded the exposed shores of all those islands. It created waves that the big-wave surfers only dream about. The brunt of that storm, having passed Hawaii, now approached the northwest coastline, pushing large schools of surface fish before its might, with the combined waves and wind action driving them closer and closer to shore.

Nor was I aware that the sea lion population already had produced a record number of pups, returning in droves. Also, large schools of salmon and steelhead were just off shore. If I had been observant, I would have noticed numerous small fish breaking the surface of the ocean, driven upward by other ones, a sign that predator fish were present. I was aware that the water where I surfed was murky, but did not understand the significance of discoloration. The flooding of nearby Elk Creek carried mud and debris into the ocean attracting sharks and other scavengers.

But perhaps most critical was my failure to read the morning paper, with its grisly account of an attack on a large bull sea lion in Tillamook Bay 30 miles to the south. Two fishermen had witnessed an attack, reporting that a large shark tossed the several-hundred-pound sea lion about as if it had been a toy, then tore off chunks of its body and devoured it before their eyes!

I had only one thing on my mind that afternoon as I left the job site—getting home to give my friend Bird the news about quitting my job. I hoped we might catch a few waves before dark.

As I pulled up to his house in Seaside, I was happy to see Jack's car in the driveway. I honked and shouted, "Hey, Bird! Come on, let's go!"

The front door of the small house opened and a blond head popped out.

"Just wait 'til I put my suit on!" he yelled, waving as he slid back inside.

He rushed out, carrying his booties, a hood, and a sandwich he had just made.

"Wanna go in my car?" Jack asked, pausing at my window, which was partially rolled down.

"No, I've got a better heater."

The Decision

"Okay. Let me grab my board."

Jack kept up a steady stream of chatter on the short drive to the point. We arrived to find only a few surfers in the water, all getting nice long rides. The waves peeled off, a clean four to five feet. Other than air temperature about 30 degrees, and water temperature about 50 degrees, conditions were ideal.

Jack grabbed his board and headed down the cliff, leaving me alone as I pulled on my suit and booties, then waxed my board. Neither of us wanted to waste one second of the remaining daylight.

By the time I had paddled out, Jack was already dropping into his first wave. I gave a loud shout of encouragement as he dropped in down the glassy face, jamming the rail, forcing him into a quick turn just under the lip. Spotting me paddling out, Jack kicked out right in front of me, sending an icy spray of water into my face.

"You'll be sorry!" I shouted, laughing as I shook the water off my face. I paddled hard to keep ahead of Bird, wanting to be first to catch the next set. "This is just what the doctor ordered," I thought, feeling my board pick up speed as I dropped in down the face of the next wave.

I was well into a clean four footer, turning my board square off the bottom, then jamming to the top where I cut back, then dragging a hand to try and hold myself back in the slot. I allowed the board to accelerate just enough to keep ahead of the white water, then kicked out. Jack caught the following wave, riding almost to the rocks lining the beach.

The two of us shared wave after wave, more than enough for us and the other four guys who were out. But eventually it had to end, with the weak winter sun edging closer to the horizon, turning a deep red and shimmering through the lips of waves as they feathered just before breaking.

"One more!" Jack shouted across the water.

I raised my hand in acknowledgment. Moments later I saw Jack paddle for an inside wave, then disappear down its face, the back of the wave blocking him from my view.

I hated to quit, but the light was rapidly fading. I glanced back at the horizon, but the gathering dusk made it difficult to see the swells. A swell rising into a good sized wave made me paddle further out.

I almost took it, but decided to paddle over, hoping for a better one outside. And, I was not disappointed—a big one peaked toward me. As the swell loomed larger and closer, I paddled hard, swinging my board around only at the last second to catch it. Only then did I really realize how little light was left. There was barely enough even to see, to ride it.

"It's now or never!" I thought, gritting my teeth and relaxing only when the tail of the board lifted. I knew I was in it, so I jumped to my feet, the wind whipping cold across my face, the water rushing past beneath my board. I was happy with the way my body reacted to hold me into the almost invisible wall of water. "This is it!", I thought, so excited that I had forgotten the depression which had gripped my mind and body a couple of hours before.

The Decision

When the wave finally began to fade out, I dropped to my stomach and guided the board to the rocks on the beach. A fire already blazed in the logs and I gratefully joined Jack and the other surfers to share its warmth.

"A great ending to a long day," I said, setting my board down. "It makes quitting my job feel like the best move I've made in a while."

CHAPTER IV

A NEW DAY 11/27/79

The sun, not yet above the horizon, was coloring the sky a pale pink, its feeble rays diffused by a mixture of icy drizzle and wet snowflakes that melted almost as soon as they touched the ground. Far out over the dark expanse of ocean floated an *anaemic* moon, slowly fading in the morning haze. A big green Cannon Beach front-end loader, black diesel smoke belching from the top of its stack, roared across the bumpy field and headed for an entrance to the deserted beach below. Albert, the driver, his heavy down jacket pulled tight around his neck, peered ahead into the space dully lighted by the vehicle's bouncing headlight beams. Each time he exhaled, a white cloud of mist formed before his face.

The driver slowed the rig, then stopped as one of the Cannon Beach police patrol cars pulled alongside, the officer sipping from a steaming cup.

"Hey!" the officer called. "What brings you out so early?"

"The high tide's been bringin' in all kinds of debris. It's keepin' us really busy just making sure the accesses stay open for the public to get to the beach. Cars wouldn't be able to drive down to Haystack if we let this stuff pile up. Come back in about twenty minutes, and you'll be able to get onto the beach."

"OK brother." the officer said, then with a quick friendly flick of his lights, drove off.

As the police car turned, its headlights picked out the road which led back up to the highway. The loader rumbled back into action, clearing a way down to a stretch of beach known by its landmark, Haystack Rock. This immense rock is one of the largest monoliths in the world, towered above the beach and surf line.

The loader scooped up a pile of debris and methodically pushed it to one side before continuing down the incline, leaving a cleared path to the beach. It was a job the operator had performed many times over the years and his hands worked the levers mechanically, without a second thought.

Then something in the sand caught his eye. He jammed on the brakes, and brought the green machine to a stop. Just at the edge of his headlight beams rose a dark mound, its shape familiar yet distorted. It did not look right. He was not quite sure what it was, but he released the brake and again began to reverse. What his headlights revealed, made him curious. He knew what it was, or at least what it had been. The big rounded form was what was left of a large sea lion.

A New Day 11/27/79

In his years of cleaning the beach, big Al had seen many dead sea lions washed up by the surf, then left to rot on the sand when the tide retreated. The difference this time was that barely half the animal remained—everything back of its front flippers was missing.

"Jesus Christ!" he muttered.

He stopped the rig and climbed down to the sand, furtively glancing out over the gloomy ocean.

The sea lion lay on its back, or what was left of its back, its inside exposed, sightless eyes staring at the cold sky, its mouth half open in a last gasp. Albert tapped it gingerly with a stick, noting the body was not yet stiff.

"Looks like you ran into one powerful eatin' machine, pal," he said again looking out to sea. "Guess we better get you outta here. We don't want to scare the hell out of the tourists!"

Pulling himself back into the rig, he went back to clearing the access before he would return to the task of disposing of the sea lion's carcass. That he would do on his way to the last beach job of the day. He fervently hoped the rest of the morning would be free from any more such grim surprises.

CHAPTER V

DAWN PATROL

I awoke momentarily out-of-it, not sure where I was. My eyes focused on the pre-dawn gloom filtering through the window, its individual panes frosted at the corners by the cold outside. Then I remembered. I had slept the night on the couch in Jack's living room. I still wondered what had awakened me so early. Then, stretching luxuriously, I remembered I no longer had to go to work.

It came again. I heard it—felt it. A low distant thundering roar that seemed to shake the house and sent a stream of adrenalin through my body. The surf was up!

"Jack!" I called. "I can hear the waves! It must have picked up."

No response. I swung into a sitting position and shivered when my feet hit the cold floor. Shivering, I pulled the blanket up around my shoulders.

"Hey, Bird!" I shouted. "Wake up!"

Finally my efforts were rewarded with a muffled, unintelligible response from his room. I walked to the door, still clutching the blanket around me, nearly tripping over one corner which dragged along the floor. I reached inside the door and flicked Jack's light on and off.

"Let's go Bird, before the crowd."

Two eyes peeked through a mop of blond hair beneath the heavy blankets. "Yeah. Okay," Jack replied, then promptly disappeared back beneath the covers.

"Do you wanna eat before we go?" I asked, throwing a pillow at the huddled mound in the bed.

Jack's head reappeared. "Sure. Look in the cupboard for some pancake mix. There isn't any butter, so we'll have to cover them with peanut butter and honey."

"Sounds good to me," I said. "I'll heat some water for coffee."

"You just said the magic word," Jack said, tossing back the covers and crawling out of bed. "I'll take mine black."

A half hour later we were on the road. I was driving my old Ford pickup toward the point. When we arrived, a couple of guys were already in the water surfing, even though the waves seemed to be jumbled by the swell direction.

I brought the truck to a stop at a spot where Jack and I could check it out before deciding to go out.

"What do you think?" I asked, breaking the silence.

"It's got size," Jack responded, "but I was hoping it would be cleaner."

"Yeah," I agreed. "How about we go south?" Jack nodded, so I started the engine, and we headed for Cannon Beach.

The morning air was crisp and cold, the coastline stretching empty as far as the eye could see, the beach virtually deserted at that early hour. To the left, green forested hills rose abruptly from the highway, their peaks touching the pale blue sky and partially shading the road from the morning sun.

We enjoyed the drive south on Route 101. The morning was beautiful and I was free to do as I wanted. It was a pleasant surprise to find the access road to the beach had been cleared, making it easy to drive down on the sand in front of Haystack Rock. The huge monolith loomed impressively from the sea, dwarfing the two surfers riding on waves below it.

"This is more like it," I said, my eyes eagerly following a surfer as he dropped down the face of a four footer. I watched as the guy kicked out just before the wave collapsed, the rising sun glinting off the smooth polished bottom of his board.

"What do you think, Bird?"

"Not bad. Not bad," Jack answered, "but before we decide, let's check out Silver Point."

"What!" I laughed. "We'll be spending the whole day just driving back and forth hoping to find a better break." Still chuckling, I restarted the engine, relieved as always when it sputtered into life.

Back on the highway we drove the few minutes to Silver Point then parked on the lookout some hundred and fifty feet above the beach. From there the coastline stretched for more than a hundred miles, the blue of the Pacific Ocean, unruffled except for the long white lines of surf rolling up onto the beach. The dark green hills rising behind the beach were illuminated by the sun, which accentuated the deep blue of the ocean. It was like looking at a postcard.

Though the view was inspiring, it was the surf intrigued us. As we watched, it became apparent it was not as clean as Haystack.

"Let's go back." I said, then snidely continued, "Or do you want to keep driving around?"

"Haystack." Jack said, smiling and giving me a jab on the shoulder.

View looking down on Haystack Rock *(Sam Foster)*

I pulled out from the lookout, drove back to Haystack Rock, and parked just above the beach. We jumped out and began the process of putting on our wetsuits. While I paused to zip mine up I took a quick glance at the waves. I noticed the two surfers we had seen earlier were inside the break and paddling for shore.

"Hey," I said, "how come they're leaving when it looks like it's getting better?"

"You can hang out here and B.S. all you want," Bird said. "Most likely they are going to work. Some people still work, not like someone I know." Jack grabbed his board and gloves. "I'm going surfing."

"Yeah," I answered thoughtfully. "I'll be right behind you." I paused to pick up the glove I had dropped, then hurried across the frozen sand to catch up with Jack, but slowed when I recognized Bruce, one of the two surfers heading for their car.

"Hey," I shouted, "How come you guys are leaving?"

"I saw something in the water," he yelled back. "We're gonna check out the point."

"What'd he see?" I called, curious at what it might be. I got no answer though. They were getting into their car and were too far away to hear my voice.

"Kenny," shouted Jack from knee deep water, "You surfing with me or not?"

Most guys like to surf with a buddy. You can never be sure when your board might whip around and bonk you on the head. If no one is there to help, you could drown.

"Yeah, yeah," I called, picking up speed as I jogged into the water.

Pausing, my feet just into the water, I pulled on my gloves. Pounding footsteps from behind made me turn just in time to see Josh, another friend, rush by at full speed. He dove through the air, his board held beneath him to cushion the landing as he launched off the top of a small wave, then skimmed across the surface of the water. When he began to slow, he paddled hard to make it over the next wave before it broke. Seeing Josh flash by pushed me to follow his example. Running through the ankle-deep water, then holding my board under me, I dove over a small wave and skimmed across the water. Paddling hard, I was able to punch through a curling wave just behind my two friends.

Even though Jack was first into the lineup, Josh was in a better position to catch the first wave. We watched in admiration as he ripped the face apart, then cranked off a bottom turn, then skated off the shoulder.

Another wave came in with Jack in perfect position as he dropped in, making it look so easy. He also ripped the wave apart, as I hoped to do on the next one.

Jack and Josh are two of Oregon's best surfers. I considered myself lucky to be surfing with them.

Now it was my turn as I sat by myself in the lineup waiting.

A nice peak formed and I turned around and paddled a few strokes. The next thing I knew I was into a clean four footer.

Jack had let me borrow his brand new surfboard that morning and I wasn't sure how I would react with it. But, it worked great and I got a great ride.

Jack and Josh were paddling back out and hooted at me as I kicked out. I felt so stoked.

I paddled back out to the rip, watching the guys catch their waves, finally reaching the lineup only to meet Steve, another buddy, paddling out.

He paddled right over by me and we were talking about how good the waves were. He said Al, our friend, was on his way out too.

Joking, I told him, "The next good wave that comes, I'm gonna get it!" He laughed and said "Yeah, yeah—okay."

Here came another nice peak. The left looked good, so I dropped in backside.

I got a nice long ride, but it closed out on the inside. As I kicked out and began paddling back out, I hoped the next set would be as good. The day had started off like a dream. In fact everything had gone great since making the decision to quit work yesterday.

 # CHAPTER VI

THE ATTACK

I paddled out alone through the ice-cold beach break, paddling hard not only to keep my blood circulating but to get back out to the lineup. As I paddled toward the four others, I relived the ride I had just taken. Stoked by the feeling, I couldn't wait to catch another one.

I could see Josh and Al paddling out in the rip next to the north side of Haystack. Steve and Jack were also visible, sitting on their boards, shivering while they waited for the next good set. We all were totally unaware that one of nature's great predators had just circled the outside rim of the rock and had glided beneath them as it moved swiftly, noiselessly, in a direction parallel to the shore.

It is impossible to know why the creature ignored the four surfers as it passed beneath them. I guess, since I was paddling hard to make it through the already crashing wave, the shark was attracted by the outline of my body as the sun shone through the water. Most likely my wetsuit-covered legs and my black-gloved hands moving rhythmically through the water made me resemble a sea lion, a Great White's favorite meal.

There was no warning. Floating on his board about fifty feet away, Steve stared in total disbelief as a mass of light gray rose out of the water, back arching, mouth agape, gill slits flapping, pectoral fins horizontal, and rows of razor-sharp teeth exposed. Paralyzed with terror, he watched helplessly as the shark instantly grabbed me and submerged me under the surface.

Oddly, I was not at first fully aware of the danger. I heard a muffled roar as the shark's massive jaws clamped across my back, pressing the board into my chest. Puzzled at what was happening, but feeling no pain, I thought I was being attacked by a sea lion. The shark pulled me two feet under water, but couldn't hold me under due to the buoyancy of the surfboard. The great white's jaw was wide enough to cover an area from my armpit to the middle of my buttocks in a half-pie shape a mere half inch away from my spine.

Not yet fully aware of what was happening, I felt tremendous pressure on my chest and heard ribs snapping and the crunching of the underside on my board as the shark turned out to sea. I felt totally helpless, as my entire body was lifted high above the water, then slammed back down beneath the surface as the shark attempted to rip and tear my body apart, its usual method of killing and eating its prey. However, the buoyancy of the board kept it from diving deep. If the shark had been able to keep me under the water, it probably would have drowned me.

The Attack

Steve and Jack were scared out of their minds. They knew exactly what was happening. I still thought it was an angry sea lion, many of which were annoyed by surfers around Haystack Rock chasing away the fish they generally fed on.

Feeling no pain and being totally helpless, I could not determine what was happening until the shark turned on its right side and allowed me a full view of its long, massive, silver-gray body and huge dorsal and pectoral fins. Only then did I know what had me! Terror-stricken, I watched its five-foot-long pectoral fin break the surface, followed by the waving of its tail fin some 15 feet behind. I could not take my eyes off of it as it surged back and forth, beating the water into a froth.

It finally dawned on me that I was in the process of being eaten by a gigantic shark, exactly as I had seen in the movie *Jaws!*

The shark continued to violently shake me back and forth as a dog would with a bone or rag doll. I could hear Steve screaming a warning at Jack. Both were too paralyzed with fear to do more than watch their friend being devoured by a shark. When my eyes met Steve's he was paddling for shore. He knew there was nothing he could do and so did I.

"Help me! Help me! Please, help!"

Defenseless, beyond anyone's help, I continued to struggle impotently, trying to twist loose, hitting the shark on its head. I was taken back under, fully expecting to see the lower half of my body ripped off and float away.

For the third time the shark lifted me high out of the water, shaking me unmercifully as I pounded its head with my fist. I could see its silver tail thrashing the water, my body snapping so hard, I was sure this was it. It seemed my life was at an end. The mauling began to subside and I made eye contact with Jack, still sitting on his board, his mouth agape and his eyes wide with horror.

When he heard me scream, the spell was broken and he began to paddle away, at the same time shouting a warning to Josh and Al who had paddled out in the rip still unaware of the attack.

"Go back! Get out of the water! Kenny is being attacked by a huge shark!" They paused "I'm not kidding you. A shark's got him."

By then Steve was paddling like crazy for shore, not realizing he was on a collision course with the shark and me. Luckily, Steve looked up in time to change his direction. Now he was even more terrified, expecting at any moment to find himself under attack.

Josh and Al heard the yelling but continued to paddle out toward the surf, not yet understanding the danger they were in. Finally, they both saw what was happening.

"Jesus," mumbled Josh at last seeing the shark. He yanked his board around and paddled to the beach, thinking that the shark might block his way.

"Holy shit! Look, Al! Do you see that? Let's get the hell outta here," shouted Josh. Al, having finally noticed, paddled his kneeboard with all his might, adrenalin feeding his muscles. Neither expected to make it to shore without a confrontation with the shark. The beach seemed to take forever to reach.

The Attack

There was no way I could blame any of them for leaving me. There was absolutely nothing, under the circumstances any of them could have done for me. I had a terrible feeling of abandonment, being left alone in the ocean, locked in the jaws of a shark. All I could do was to beat my fists and scream, praying in my mind, watching my life pass before me, sure I was dead meat. Worst of all was the sadness I felt, knowing I would never again see my sons.

Later I estimated the shark held me in its jaws for about twenty seconds. It seemed closer to an hour, the longest short period of my life. Then suddenly, the pressure was released and I was floating on the surface of the ocean about twenty feet from my surfboard. My surf leash, made out of half-inch bungie chord, had snapped like a piece of thread. I could not believe my luck. Still terrified, I looked all around for the shark. It had disappeared below the surface. I fully expected it to hit me again. A circle of blood-red water surrounded me as I treaded water about 100 yards from the beach.

The fear of another attack pumped a charge of adrenalin into my bloodstream, giving me the strength to swim the twenty feet to my board and pull myself on top of it. Blood poured from my wounds, enlarging the circle of blood around me. I was surprised to find my legs and arms still attached and that I was not paralyzed.

Drawing strength from an unknown source, I paddled like a madman, legs bent at the knees, feet as high as I could hold them. My primary fear was that a second attack would sever them from my body. I gasped for air between sobs of fear, expecting at any second to feel the shark's jaws clamp down on my body and pull me back to sea to die alone.

I could hear myself pleading, as I kept moving my arms, "Let me see my sons again. Please God, let me see them again."

Although I felt no pain, I knew I had been badly hurt. Blood ran down my arms and over my hands as I paddled. I could hear myself breathing through the rip in my back, a mixture of air and blood gurgling in and out with each breath. It sounded like the noise made when you squeeze a nearly empty ketchup bottle. I was afraid to touch my back or try to look at it, knowing if I saw my own blood gushing out, I would pass out and never make it back to shore.

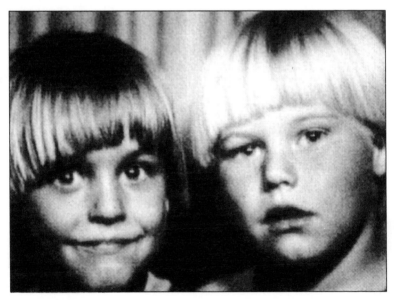

My sons, Jeremy-4, Justin-3 *(Kenny Doudt)*

The Attack

A crashing sound behind me sent a wave of terror through my body. I expected to feel the shark's teeth sink into my legs, but instead was relieved when I looked over my right shoulder and it was a wave breaking, its force lifting the rear end of my board and pushing me toward the beach. The foam from the crashing wave was a deep red. I had only enough strength to grab the rails with my hands and hold on with all my might, leaving my deliverance to the power of the ocean.

My own strength finally deserted me. My head drooped to the board, and my arms dragged limply alongside. My only hope was that I had gotten into water too shallow for the shark to follow.

Josh, Jack, and Al, standing at the water's edge, stared in disbelief as the dwindling wave pushed me in their direction. None had given me the slightest chance of surviving the brutal attack by the biggest shark any of them had ever seen. The foam on either side of me was red and was a fading trail out to sea.

Steve, who had reached the beach first, had paused only long enough to unstrap his surf leash, then race across the sand to phone for help, knowing he had to do all he could to save my life after what he had just seen.

I felt the sand rub against my finger tips as the wave subsided in less than knee deep water. I was too weak to lift my head or to move even my fingers. Blood bubbled from ribs and wounds all along my back. The sound of air rushing in and out with each breath scared me worse than anything else. Oddly,

I had not lost consciousness, nor felt much pain. All I felt was relief that I had made it to shore.

Now, out of the monster's reach, I was ready to die.

 # CHAPTER VII

THE RESCUE

Josh, Jack and Al began to draw the attention of the people on the cliff above, especially surfers just about to head for the ocean.

Two whose attention was immediately caught were Tom and Mike, who were just pulling on their wetsuits at Mike's girlfriend's house above Haystack Rock.

Tom pointed at the growing crowd below. "Isn't that a surfer in trouble just inside the white water? He must be badly hurt. I can see blood in the water around him."

"Jesus. I wonder who it is?" Asked Mike.

"Gotta be someone we know," Tom answered.

"Let's get down there and see if we can help."

The two rushed from the house, jumping into Mike's car, slamming the doors shut as they roared off down to the beach.

Al, Jack and Josh, without any thought that they might be in danger if the shark followed me into the shallow water, rushed to my aid. The water around me was deep red. No one thought I could possibly live after losing the amount of blood which was pouring out of the numerous wounds across my back. The flow was only partially stemmed by the tattered remnants of my wetsuit. When they got to me, they could see white rib ends protruding through torn flesh as they turned me on my side. What appeared to be gallons of blood poured from the inside of my wetsuit, turning the water an even darker red.

"Jesus," exclaimed Al. "We gotta get him out of the water before the shark gets him again!"

They could actually see exposed organs pulsating beneath broken ribs. My heart, with each contraction, shot spurts of blood from the severed ends of arteries. They worried that if they picked me up face down, as I still lay on the board, they might force the ragged ends of ribs into other organs and do further injury to me. Instead they rolled me onto my back, face up, and grabbed my arms and legs to lift me off the board. Fighting their way through the shallow water and surf, the three tried their best to keep both my body and head above the water. Everyone worried with each step that the shark might attack again.

I had remained fully conscious since the shark's first savage onslaught, but now felt myself slipping, beginning to drift into unconsciousness, sure that I was dying with no chance to survive, Al and Josh had each grabbed an arm, but Jack, who was holding my legs, had not stopped to take off his surf leash, and was dragging his board through the water behind him. When the fin dug in and caught, it tripped him and he stumbled. He lost his grip on my legs and causing everyone to stumble. My back whacked into the sand! He felt bad about it, but it may have saved my life. The jolt, like a slap in the face, brought me back to consciousness, reinvigorating my will to live. All I had wanted was to get to the beach before I died.

"Come on you guys," I thought to myself. "Take it easy, be gentle. I'm hurt bad."

I was again conscious, aware of Jack reaching down to undo the leash from his ankle, then again grabbing my other leg. The three lifted me above the water and struggled to get me up onto the dry sand, where they laid me on my right side.

Watching the entire episode from a big house perched on top of the cliff above Haystack Rock was Dallas McKennon, a movie actor. He had been checking out the surf through binoculars when he noticed three men struggling through the surf carrying what appeared to him to be an injured surfer. Fine-focusing his lenses he could see blood in the water around us. He felt the man they carried was either dead or very badly injured. Realizing something serious had occurred, he dropped his glasses to the table, stepped around the blazing wood stove that warmed his house, grabbed the phone and dialed "9-1-1".

"Send an ambulance to the beach in front of Haystack Rock. It looks like a surfer has been badly injured." After hanging up, he rushed out his door and charged down the bluff.

In Seaside, eight miles north, Sam, a local free-lance photographer, was in his darkroom developing a series of pictures he had taken of a lighthouse from a helicopter. As was his habit, he had his E.R. radio scanner on, keeping him in touch with potential news stories. He liked to get a head start on photographing events for the local papers. His ears perked up when he heard the caller excitedly request an ambulance and paramedics to aid an injured surfer on the beach near Haystack Rock. Within minutes he was driving south on Highway 101, his cameras and equipment, as always, carefully packed in the trunk of his car, ready for any emergency, or photographable event.

At about the same time the phone jangled in the usually quiet Cannon Beach Fire Department which housed the city ambulance and paramedic base station. It was on its third ring when Gary, one of the paramedics, shouted from the kitchen where he was preparing breakfast, "Hey, get the phone, please."

He was carrying two cups of steaming coffee when the excited voice of his partner stopped him in his tracks.

"No kidding!" exclaimed Jim, a look of shock on his face. "We're on our way."

He almost knocked the coffee cups out of Gary's hands as he rushed to the ambulance and yanked open the driver's door. The engine roared. The ambulance was already moving when Gary jumped in.

Ray, the relief paramedic, was digging clams along the beach about a mile south of Haystack Rock when his belt beeper went off. He had just dug a gigantic razor clam from the wet sand. Shaking his head at the annoying interruption, he dropped it into the clam sack and raced across the sand to his truck where he radioed in for a report. Shaking his head in disbelief he jumped in his rig and proceeded to the scene a mile north.

In the meantime, unaware that Dallas had already phoned for help, Steve, one of the surfers, winded from running across the beach and up the bluff, pounded on the door of the first house he came to. It was the downstairs half of a duplex. When no one answered, he tried the door and found it locked. He raced upstairs to the second-story apartment. Again no one answered his knock, but he could see a wall phone through the open curtains of a window. A big dog was standing in the middle of the room barking up a storm!

Frantic, he tried the door handle and found it unlocked. Entering slowly, he stared into the fangs of the growling dog. Scared, with the hair standing up on the back of his neck, he walked sidewise past the dog, who continued to growl as he backed to where the phone was. Staring the dog down, Steve reached out and grabbed the phone. He was too excited to remember "9-1-1", so dialed "0" instead for the operator.

"May I help you?" the operator asked, in a casual voice.

"Quick, send an ambulance down to Haystack Rock in Cannon Beach," he gasped.

"You must dial "9-1-1" for an emergency."

"Please do it for me," Steve pleaded, his hand shaking so badly he could not possibly dial. Also, his hands were still numb from surfing in the frigid water. "My friend has just been attacked by a giant shark, and there's a dog in here ready to chew me up!"

"A shark attack?" she said, this time in a voice that shook.

"Yes. Kenny Doudt," Steve's voice rising as he was still gasping for breath from his long run.

"Just settle down," the operator said in a calming voice. "I'll notify paramedics immediately."

"Thanks." Steve dropped the phone in its cradle, still staring into the intimidating eyes of the growling dog. He backed toward the door. Tripping over a throw rug, he stumbled and almost fell down. The dog lunged, his mouth snapping shut less than an inch from Steve's arm. Stepping quickly through the door, he slammed it on the dog just as it made its second lunge. He could see it through the window as it barked and clawed the inside of the door. As he rushed down the steps, he could still hear the dog frantically scratching and barking as he ran to his truck. He raced to the fire station to make sure help was on its way.

Gary maneuvered the speeding ambulance through the cars along the road, red lights flashing, siren screaming. An operator came on the radio, her voice excited as she informed them that the emergency was a shark attack at Haystack Rock.

"Jesus Christ!" Gary said reaching over to turn up the volume on the siren. "Did you hear that?"

He accelerated the medic wagon to the maximum speed, still weaving in and out of traffic.

Steve, seeing and hearing the racing paramedics, flashed his lights and honked his horn to get their attention. He shouted out his open window and pointing down at Haystack Rock. He saw Gary nod in acknowledgment, then slow the ambulance for the turn down the beach.

Steve almost caused an accident when he made a U-turn in front of oncoming traffic, his tires spewing gravel as he fishtailed back onto the road, racing after the ambulance. Then he almost rammed into it when it slowed for a curve in the access above the sand. He was breathing in gasps, tears blinding his eyes, his stomach knotted with fear that his friend might already be dead. He could not believe anyone could live after being so badly mauled.

Sam, the photographer, heard the same emergency call that the ambulance heard—a surfer near Haystack Rock had been attacked by a shark. Sucking in his breath he increased his speed, wishing he had a siren as he met the traffic in Cannon Beach. He had been successfully selling photographs to local papers and magazines, but to be the first on the scene of a shark attack incident might get his pictures onto UPI or even on television.

As I lay on my side before the medics arrived, I felt increasing pain with each breath, making it impossible not to moan. My obvious increasing pain scared Jack, who ran off for help, leaving me in Josh's care. It had been a couple of minutes since they carried me from the water, but to Josh it seemed like hours. I could hear him praying out loud as he held me on my side, begging God to let me live.

I was still on my side when Tom and Mike's car skidded to a stop not ten feet from where I lay. Josh, his skin ashen, tried valiantly to hold the torn flaps of flesh closed over the wounds, hoping to slow the bleeding. He was still praying, with Tom and Mike now at his side. Tom looked at Mike after seeing the blood ooze from between Josh's fingers.

They felt there was no way I could survive. The sand beneath me was already soaked with blood from the gaping wound which ran the length of my back.

Tom and Mike stared out into the ocean expecting once again to see a dorsal fin appear above the surface.

Tom knelt beside Josh using both of his hands to help hold the wound closed, Mike, seeing there was little he could do, ran to his car for a towel. The *used ones* Josh had were already soaked with blood. They covered my wound, then leaned close to my ear telling me, "Hang in there, bro. You're gonna make it."

"You're gonna be okay, Kenny," Josh sobbed. "I know you are."

Tom took hold of my gloved hand, rubbing the skin to warm it. He then rubbed my legs and arms through the wetsuit, hoping that would keep me from going into shock.

"Tom," I whispered. "Please take off my gloves,"

Tom started to do as I had asked, then stopped, deciding they would help keep me warmer. Even though they were all sure I was dying, they worked their hardest to keep me as warm and comfortable as possible for what they thought were the last few minutes of my life. They could hear me mumble, but were unable to understand what I was trying to say. Everyone was surprised I was still conscious and talking.

The Rescue

Josh was unaware of the crowd that had gathered. People pressed in close to get a better look at my wounds. One of those gathered was Mike's girlfriend, a registered nurse. She took one look at me, and shook her head without much hope, "The best thing we can do for him is to keep him warm. Does anyone have a blanket?"

"Yeah, we do," said a young lady, who grabbed her boyfriend's arm and ran down the beach to get it. They returned a minute later, carrying an old army blanket.

"Hold it up to break the wind," ordered the R.N. An icy wind was whipping across the sand, raising goose bumps on those standing there watching.

"May I be of assistance?" a tourist inquired.

"Sure," answered Steve, handing him a corner of the blanket used to shield me from the wind. He took it and inquisitively lowered one corner to take a peek at my wounds. Looking down on the torn and bleeding flesh and protruding ribs, he dropped the blanket, fell to his knees, vomiting uncontrollably, until someone helped him to his feet and away from the scene.

I tried to block out the terrible pain which engulfed my body by thinking of my sons, Jeremy and Justin. I knew that if I did not fight to live, I would never see them again. The distant scream of a siren raised my spirits. There was no way I was going to give up. I had to see my boys again, and tell them how much I loved them. I had too much to live for to let go.

CHAPTER VIII

THE AMBULANCE TRIP TO SEASIDE HOSPITAL

"Slow down, Gary!" Jim shouted over the scream of the siren.

"I hope it's been cleared," Gary said slowing the ambulance down to enter the beach access. "I saw some people stuck a couple of days ago."

"We may have to use four wheel drive," Jim suggested.

"No, it looks like it's been cleared." Gary let the ambulance roll through, then speeded up when he got on the flat hard packed sand. "It's hard to believe a guy could get attacked by a shark so far north. I guess it's all the rain and heavy river runoff, and maybe there was a school of steelhead offshore, still in school."

"Who knows?" Jim said pointing, ahead toward the people who were crowded around me. "The poor guy was in the wrong place at the wrong time, or maybe the right place at the wrong time, I don't know."

"Man!" Jim exclaimed. "Look at the size of that crowd already gathered."

"It's a good thing other surfers were out to help him."

"I'm going to honk the horn,"

The crowd slowly divided, for the ambulance, leaving only a narrow lane, Gary jammed his hand down on the horn, hitting one last blast on the siren at the same time.

My spirits rose when I heard the siren get louder and louder. I felt, when I heard the tires slapping across the hard packed sand and the crowd grow quiet, that I might make it after all. I had come to the conclusion that the only thing keeping me alive were my eyes, I thought that if I let them close, I would never open them again. I began to feel safe when the ambulance stopped close to where I lay.

Both paramedics were surprised when Sam aimed his camera at them. He caught them again as they pulled the stretcher out of the back and set it on the sand beside me.

"How'd Sam get here so quick?" mumbled Gary as he leaned down to fold back the sheet covering the stretcher.

"You know Sam," Jim answered. "He always has his emergency scanner on, even when he's taking a shower." Jim, looking back up from the stretcher grinning, shouted at the crowd, "Please move back. We need more room."

The crowd moved quickly.

Gary dropped to his knees, setting the already opened first aid kit next to me. Josh, still holding me, explained to Gary what had just happened. Concerned, he pulled aside the blood-soaked towel covering the gaping wounds. The crowd gasped when they saw the wounds, but again pressed close, leaning over the medics to get a closer look. Gary shook his head as he moved his fingers up and down my arm trying to find a pulse.

"We gotta get him to the hospital quick, and I mean quick!" Gary said, helping Jim to slide me onto the stretcher. Again Sam's camera went off in their faces.

"How about moving your head so I can get a closeup of the wound?" Sam asked, almost tripping Gary as he stepped around him.

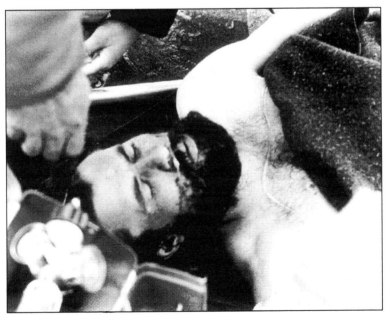

Paramedics- saving my life *(Sam Foster)*

"We've got a guy dying, and you want him to pose for pictures!"

They told Sam to back off out of the way. They moved the stretcher around to work on me. Nevertheless he continued to take pictures.

By that time, Ray, a third paramedic, had arrived and immediately joined in trying to keep me alive. The first thing they did was to set up a nasal cannula for administration.

"How's his blood pressure?"

"What pressure?" "There is no pressure, the pulse is thready and barely palpable."

"I can't believe he's still alive."

"Hypothermia." He answered.

"His body temperature has dropped below ninety degrees."

"Pulse is weak and very irregular. We gotta get blood into this guy and get him warmed up. Otherwise he'll arrest."

Hearing the paramedics discuss my wounds and what they needed to do didn't bother me until I heard my suit being cut off. It was worth a good $250.

"Get some blankets out and let's get this guy warmed up."

I could do nothing but listen. The slicing off of my wetsuit worried me more about how much it had cost than I was afraid about losing my life. The suit was only a couple of months old, but at least thinking about it kept my mind off of dying. I could not tell who said it, but I heard a voice say, "Stick in an I.V."

Next I felt myself being lifted as they pulled my wetsuit from beneath, then a coolness as my wounds became exposed. The next sensation was a slight pressure around my torso when the paramedics placed trauma dressings over the area to protect me and slow the bleeding. My legs were lifted onto the MAST trousers. They closed the velcro around my legs. I felt the pressure on my legs as they pumped them up, which allowed what remaining blood I had to be more available to my vital organs. By then, I was covered with blankets to help retain my body heat.

The medics were annoyed by Sam and his camera as they lifted the stretcher into the ambulance.

"Jesus," Ray said "Come on, don't take any more pictures."

Sam moved back, then leaned around to get a last shot before the back door closed. He took a last look at the back of the ambulance, then cocked his camera and turned to Steve and Jack, hoping to get some more pictures while he had them on the beach.

Jim jumped in and started the engine while Gary and Ray got into the back to work on keeping me alive, a task they both thought hopeless. One or the other kept asking me questions, trying to keep me alert while checking the I.V., tubes, oxygen and monitoring equipment. Jim steered the vehicle back across the sand and up the access to the main road with the siren screaming.

The paramedics had barely pulled away when Sam turned to Steve and Jack asking them what had happened.

"Listen," Jack said. "We gotta get to the hospital. Josh and Al are already on their way."

Steve & Jack, terrified, with my Surfboard *(Sam Foster)*

"Do me a favor," Sam asked. "Can I take some photos? I need one of Kenny's board. Can you hold it up for me please?" I want to get a picture of the bite marks. Maybe I can take the board back to my lab and get some closeups."

Sam started to walk over to Jack and Steve. Jack said, "The board is mine and Kenny just borrowed it for this morning session."

Sam began snapping pictures of them pointing out to sea, holding up the board and looking at the bite marks.

"How about one more, for the press," said Sam lifting his camera to his eye and fiddling with the fine focus.

"That's enough!" Jack said. "He was our good friend."

Sam shrugged as he shot a couple of last pictures of Jack and Steve collecting the pieces of wetsuit off the sand.

"Hey, you guys," shouted Sam as they left. "Hope you aren't mad. I'm just doing my job. The media will be clamoring for pictures. I feel bad about Kenny getting bitten too."

Steve and Jack acknowledged Sam's explanation, then trotted across the sand to Steve's car.

People still stood on the beach talking about the attack, some pointing out to sea, others searching the surface, expecting to see a dorsal fin. All were relieved they had not been in the water when the attack had occurred. Sam snapped off a few shots of the crowd and of Haystack Rock. Satisfied, he ran to his car. His hope was to get the film developed as quickly as possible, then drive the pictures to Portland. He was sure that the press would pay to buy everything he had.

In the meantime, the ambulance roared through the streets of Cannon Beach, the siren screaming, cars pulling over to get out of the way, people leaning out of windows and doorways to see what the noise was all about.

Jim grabbed the radio microphone and called ahead to warn the Seaside Hospital emergency staff to get prepared for a major trauma. "We've got a surfer who has been badly mauled by a large shark in the ocean off Haystack Rock."

"Yeah, okay we'll be ready for him." Jim looked at Ray and said "I don't think she takes us seriously!"

Continuing on the radio, Jim said, "This is for real." "The victim has a deep laceration on the left side of his body running from just below his armpit to the middle of his buttocks, extending across his back almost to his spine. There is also a major laceration across his left buttock. That's how deep the laceration is. He has lost most of his blood. You can see his ribs. His flesh is laid back in a four to six inch strip. This guy is in real bad shape!"

Jim could feel himself getting excited, his voice rising several decibels with each sentence.

"Just have the E.R. ready! His vitals are poor. You'll need lots of blood. He can't have much left and he's still losing it."

Although I could hear them talking, I had begun to feel I was going to make it. Being in the hands of the paramedics gave me faith that I would live. I still could not believe what had happened to me. There was not great pain, just a feeling of weakness. The only uncomfortable sensation was the terrible cold throughout my body.

The Ambulance Trip to Seaside Hospital

Growing weaker, having lost at least six pints of blood and suffering from extreme hypothermia, I was barely aware of the paramedics working on me. Cold permeated every portion of my body. As uncomfortable as the cold made me, I later learned that it was the hypothermia that slowed down my bodily functions, a major reason why I am still alive.

The ambulance ride to Seaside Hospital seemed so fast. My only annoyance was the continual and repetitious questioning by the paramedics. They would ask my name, then how I spelled it. Next they would ask my age, my weight, my address, the names of my kids, my friends. As soon as I got through that, they would start again. Then, without warning, the siren went silent, making me apprehensive that my end was near. I calmed down when I finally realized we were at the hospital and the ambulance was backing up to the E.R. entrance.

The next thing I remember was seeing the ambulance door being yanked open. The head doctor of the emergency room appeared and immediately began barking out orders. Paramedics, uniformed nurses and orderlies rushed about doing his bidding. I felt a jolt as paramedics slid the stretcher out and dropped the wheels to the concrete. Since I could feel and hear things happening, I knew I was still alive. I was aware of being rolled down a hallway, people rushing along beside me holding up bottles attached by rubber tubes to various parts of my body.

"Somebody get a sample of his blood so we can cross-match it," I heard the E.R. doctor order.

Almost immediately a needle was inserted into one of my veins. The nurse began to worry when it took so long to fill the syringe. Dr. Wayne was now being paged over a loudspeaker ordering him to the emergency room.

"He is in the middle of a double hernia operation," a nurse said. "It will be several minutes before he is finished in the operating room."

The E.R. doctor cracked out an order that the carpet layer who had cut off two fingers would have to be moved out of E.R. to make room for me.

"There's nothing that can be done for him anyway until his partner returns with the cut-off fingers," said a voice.

The poor man was disturbed at being forced to vacate the operating table until he caught a glimpse of my torn back as they wheeled me in. A nurse told him "Look at this guy, and it might help the pain you're in."

I was beginning to feel severe pain in several places and I was becoming worried at the apparent confusion in the emergency room. I could hear blaring orders for more supplies and equipment. Requests were made for more medical help. I felt a nurse insert a new I.V. so they could pump blood back into my still bleeding body. It was either replace the blood faster than it was running out or there was no chance I could be saved.

"Try to relax," I heard the E.R. doctor say. "I'm going to insert a chest tube into your lung to make your breathing easier."

The Ambulance Trip to Seaside Hospital

I relaxed as best I could, feeling something press into my rib cage, the pressure repeated again before the doctor succeeded in getting the tube between my ribs into my left lung.

Finally Dr. Wayne had another doctor relieve him on the double hernia operation and rushed to the emergency room where most of the nurses and the emergency doctor were covered with my blood which continued to seep and spurt from a dozen puncture wounds. The blood transfusions were barely able to keep up with the loss.

I was still conscious and starting to feel more pain. Then I caught sight of Steve's girlfriend, Suzi, peeking over the shoulder of one of the nurses to see how I was. She worked at the hospital, but the expression on her face was pure shock and horror when she looked down at my back in total disbelief. Her hand moved involuntarily to her mouth as she staggered backward.

More nurses rushed in carrying bundles of clean gauze, while others rushed out with blood-soaked ones. A nurse entered with liter bottles of fluids on a tray. Blood was on the way to replace that which dripped from my wounds onto the operating table, then onto the floor.

Two orderlies helped Dr. Wayne roll me from my back onto my right side, exposing gashes and wounds. The doctor's voice showed his noticeable alarm as he stepped back from the table and said, "Get the Coast Guard on the phone immediately. We have to move this man to a Portland Hospital. There is no way we can handle this severe a case with the limited equipment we have here."

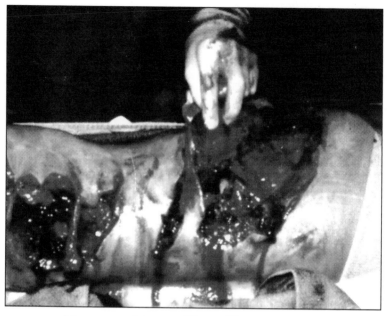

My exposed torso *(Saint Vincent Hosp.)*

Within minutes a nurse rushed into the E.R. to say, "The Coast Guard says their helicopter would not be able to make it from Astoria to Portland. There's a major snow storm over the coastal range."

"Then get an ambulance ready for us," Dr. Wayne said. "See that there is ample blood for continuing transfusion. The pressure on the MAST trousers will have to be kept high. He is still losing blood almost as fast as we can get it into him."

Nurses, orderlies, and emergency room personnel rushed about following the doctor's orders, all knowing that saving my life was down to mere seconds of time. I felt myself lifted back onto a *gurney,* then pushed out of the emergency room and down a brightly lighted corridor. While the double doors were held open two orderlies rushed me outside. A rush of cold air hit my face just before the medics and Dr. Wayne slid me back into the ambulance. I heard the roar of the engine and the tug of speed on my body as we moved forward. I began to worry there was no way we could make it in time.

CHAPTER IX

THE DRIVE TO
PORTLAND

The driver turned on the siren and accelerated away from the Seaside Hospital, beginning what would be a long tortuous drive through the coastal mountain range to Portland.

"It sure is a beautiful day," the driver said as he hit the siren and slowed for an intersection. "I never get tired of looking at the ocean."

Dr. Wayne ignored the observation as he bent close to examine the oxygen mask over my face. I was having a hard time breathing, which worried him. After taking it off and checking the air intake, he replaced it.

"Look at all the people lining the streets," the driver said, blasting the siren again. "Everyone in Seaside must have heard about the attack."

"If they want gore," the paramedic said, "they ought to go see the emergency room. There was blood everywhere — on the walls, on the floor, on the examining table."

"It's coming over the radio stations now," the driver said turning up the volume, an announcer describing the attack. He estimated the shark to be more than fifteen feet long.

I could barely understand the discussion inside the ambulance when Dr. Wayne shook my shoulder and asked, "What's your name?" He didn't want me to close my eyes.

I heard the doctor complain that he was having a hard time getting blood into my body fast enough to keep up with the blood I was still losing.

"How are you feeling?" Dr. Wayne asked again, shaking my shoulder. "Hang on, buddy. We'll be in Portland in a little while."

I knew he was trying to keep my spirits up and keep me alert. Every time I blinked, he would check the air intake from the oxygen tank. The ambulance had to keep slowing as it went around sharp mountain curves. The snow was falling faster. The wheels kept spinning on the ice each time the driver tried to accelerate around a hairpin curve. The ambulance slowed down, then stopped.

"It looks like there's been a wreck up ahead," his assistant said. "A car is upside down, partially blocking the road."

We started moving again when a bystander waved us around the wrecked car. The siren screamed the entire time as we bumped along the side of the road to get past.

"There's a bad wreck on Highway 26 about forty miles west of Portland," the driver said into the radio mike. "Better get another ambulance and the highway patrol there quick."

I felt as though I was traveling through a fairy land, with everything white outside the window I looked through. The ambulance lights spread red color across the snow. Every time I closed my eyes and began to think about my sons, the doctor would shake me and ask questions to see if I was still conscious.

The doctor reached across me to adjust the intravenous tubing, chest tube and monitoring electrodes.

"His blood pressure has dropped to zero," I heard him say.

I could tell he was worried, but to me everything was peaceful, like I was floating up to heaven. There was no pain, only a little numbness. I had full of faith that Dr. Wayne would keep me alive.

It's hard to explain my life flashing before my eyes, but oddly enough, it did happen. It was sort of like watching parts of my life on a television screen. I saw the time I almost drowned when I was only two years old, in the ocean off New Jersey, and then everything since. The part of my life that kept floating through my mind was recollections of my sons, Justin and Jeremy. I had to live, or I would never see them again.

Dr. Wayne kept shaking me out of my dream world with more questions. I could tell he was concerned by the way he kept monitoring my pulse and blood pressure. He kept increasing the pressure in the MAST trousers to force what blood I had left up from my legs into my upper torso and brain.

When my pulse increased and my blood pressure began to rise he seemed to relax a bit.

Actually, it was very peaceful, staring out the window at the white snow banks passing by. It was so serene that I really did not worry about how precarious my life was.

"How much further?" I heard Dr. Wayne ask the driver.

"We're almost out of the mountains now," he answered.

"Which hospital do you want me to head for?"

"How long is it to St. Vincent?" the doctor asked.

"Between fifteen and twenty minutes."

"Radio them that we are on our way," the doctor ordered.

I was starting to fade away again, having a hard time keeping my mind focused or my eyes open. Dr. Wayne immediately pumped more pressure into the MAST trousers, continually assuring me that I would be all right.

"We're almost at St. Vincent," I heard the driver say. "Is he gonna make it?"

"He's got to! We're too close, and he's held on for so long."

The driver cranked the siren up a few more notches and seemed to step on the gas. The ambulance was flying down the highway. I felt the ambulance turn off the highway. It then went down under an overpass to the entrance of the hospital emergency room. Doctors, nurses, and orderlies were waiting in the open doorway as the ambulance backed up to the entrance. The back door was yanked open and a rush of cold air hit me as they lifted me out, lowered the wheels on the gurney and rolled me into the hospital.

"Hang in there," Dr. Wayne said into my ear. "We made it."

I was sure that the doctors, paramedics and nurses had done everything they could to keep me alive up to this point. Now it would be up to the surgeons to put me back together.

As they rolled me down the hall, a surgeon named Dr. Starr leaned over me examining the wounds and at the same time telling me I was going to be all right.

"We are going to lift you onto the operating table," Dr. Starr said. "The nurse will give you a shot to relieve the pain."

He then grabbed my arm and moved it, mumbling something I could not understand. I was in pain. It was the first major pain I had felt because my body was warming up.

"Don't move me," I begged, tears running down my face.

"Nurse," Dr. Starr said. "Give him the shot now."

I could feel the needle slide into my arm, lessening the pain almost immediately. My life was in the absolute control of the doctors surrounding the operating table. I no longer worried, trusting in the doctors as if they were God.

The operating room had been put in full readiness for my arrival, a top surgical team of six doctors scrubbed, gowned and ready to go. Doctors Ahmad, Ham, Okubo, Matsui, Egan, and Starr were highly trained for open-heart surgery. Lucky me!

I could hear the commotion, but everything seemed to be happening in slow motion now and in muted tones. I could barely make out the figures clustered around the operating table, their voices distorted, as I slipped into unconsciousness.

I had immediately been connected to monitoring devices, screens showing all my vital signs for the doctors to read as they worked.

Once they had my vital signs under control, they examined my back and buttocks. A photographer aimed his camera at the wounds and took pictures for a medical journal. He took one shot with a doctor holding up a slab of flesh showing, the gravity of the wound.

Everyone went to work. The first stage of the operation was an exploration of my left chest cavity. Next came wound repair by surgeons Ahmad, Ham, Okubo and Matsui. The wound consisted of a gaping hole, a collapsed lung and four

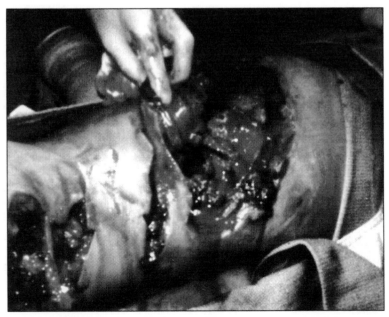

Dr. holding a slab of meat; ME! *(Saint Vincent Hosp.)*

fractured ribs. The ribs had been broken in several places and some were splintered by the shark's teeth. My back muscles hung loosely around the wound cavity and there was massive bleeding into my left lung.

After a thorough examination of the lung, heart and left hemidiaphragm, or kidney, they found no significant damage to any of those organs. The skin around the chest wound had been serrated by the shark's teeth and some of the muscles were missing.

Next, four broken ribs were rejoined. Before they could complete the repair of the ribs, the bleeding had to be brought under control. The collapsed lung was re-expanded by repair-

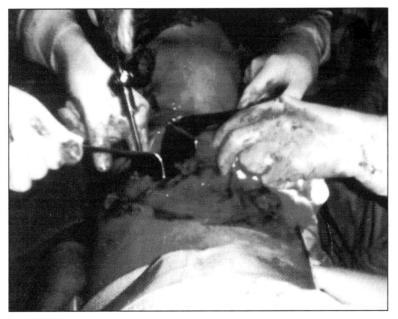

The gaping hole in my left side. *(Saint Vincent Hosp.)*

ing the broken ribs and chest wall. The bleeding arteries in the muscles overlying the torn ribs were ligated. Then the soft tissue was put in place and stitched up. Drainage tubes were left in place and connected to an underwater seal.

At this stage, the lacerations were left to Dr. Starr to repair.

The doctors participating in the next phase of the surgery were Starr, Ahmad, Ham, and Okubo. In their examination they found a jagged laceration on the left side of my torso, passing in a ragged, irregular line posteriorly and downward. The total length of this wound was approximately 14 inches. Just distal to that wound was a second such laceration of about seven inches in length.

Both wounds required considerable undermining for closure. They were deep enough to sever a portion of the "latissimus dorsi"—the main back muscle. Both wounds were repaired by Dr. Ahmad.

There was a third massive wound which was a 10-inch long, V-shaped flap based, on the lateral aspect of the left buttocks. This wound was deep enough to lacerate the "gluteus maximus" and several fragments of that muscle, as well as chunks of subcutaneous fat, were missing. All of the wounds contained what appeared to be sand, but no other foreign material.

After the chest wound had been closed by Dr. Ahmad, I was placed on my right side, and the affected areas were prepared with Betadine. Debridement of the wound edges was carried out with a number 20 scalpel and deep closure performed with a number 4-0 Vicryl. The skin was closed by interupted ethilon. A large soft rubber Penrose drain was inserted beneath each of the three separate wounds, three on the wound on the buttock. In addition, a hemovac suction tube was inserted under the lacerated portion of the "gluteous maximus." Any muscle or subcutaneous fat with questionable viability was excised. Before closing, all wounds had been repeatedly irrigated with saline solution and cleaned with 4x4 gauze pads. At the completion of the wound closures, the operative sites were covered with xeroform gauze, followed by 4x4 pads, fluffs, ABDs and Kerlix dressings.

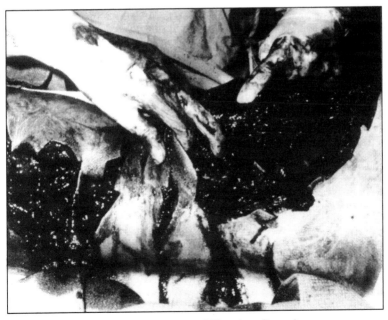

Before Surgery. *(Charles Starr)*

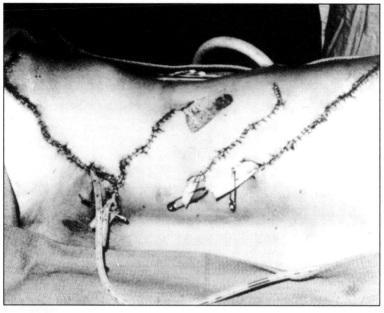

After Surgery. *(Charles Starr)*

In summary, I had suffered severe damage to four ribs smashed by the power of the shark's teeth and jaws. The monster had exerted a force of approximately 15,000 pounds per square inch in its bite. In addition, I had a punctured lung, exposed heart and kidney, shredded muscles, severed nerves, mutilation of fatty tissue and massive internal bleeding.

I had lost all but one pint of the eleven pints of blood a body generally holds. My body temperature had dropped below ninety degrees Fahrenheit, but ironically, it was the extreme hypothermia that slowed down all my bodily functions and probably saved my life.

The Drive to Portland

The shark had inflicted a half-pie-shaped wound that went from just below my armpit to the middle of my left side. According to the doctors, if the teeth had gone another half inch further toward my backbone, the spinal cord could have been severed, paralyzing me from there on down. Dr. Starr quit counting the stitches taken when he reached five hundred. Fortunately, they said I was in good enough shape that my body tolerated all these procedures well.

Once I was in stable enough condition to be moved, I was taken to intensive care. It had taken more than three hours of surgery to complete the repairs on my back and inside my chest. The doctors gathered in a room for a press conference that afternoon, before media representatives from all over the northwest.

In the meantime, back at Cannon Beach, the local media were covering the reaction of the residents to the attack. There was a big crowd just off the beach, which was not only a popular surf spot, but well known to residents and tourists alike. People had gathered to talk in the Round Table, one of the town's more popular restaurants. It got its name from the gigantic round table in the middle of the dining room which could seat 20 or more people.

None of the locals who gathered were yet ready to accept the reality of a shark attack at their beach. Most believed I had banged into a rock. Others agreed with the people on the beach just after the attack, who had said it was an angered sea lion.

Surfing with the Great White Shark

Two guys who surfed got up and looked out the window, a look of worry on their faces. Neither was sure he would ever want to surf there again.

CHAPTER X

RECOVERY IN THE HOSPITAL

November 28, 1979, the first day after the attack, I was so deeply under sedation that Dr. Ahmad had a nurse give me a shot to bring me out of it. He and the crew stood around my bed watching for signs of consciousness.

With the realization of what had been done to save me, I realized I could have been dead.

Although I was happy to be alive, pain throbbed throughout my entire body with each heartbeat, from the tips of my fingers to the ends of my toes. I really wasn't sure where I was or what had happened to me.

I hurt so badly, my body shook uncontrollably, as if I was freezing. I tried to twist around to escape the pain, but I was strapped to my bed.

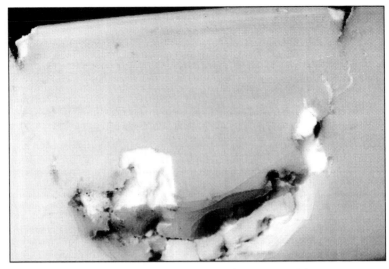

Bottom of Surfboard. *(Terry Link)*

Top of Surfboard. *(Terry Link)*

Relief came when a nurse gave me a shot of morphine. The pain began to fade away almost instantly. So did my mind, which drifted off into space.

I was aware, as I lay strapped to my bed, of the clicking noise of the life support system I was hooked up to, with small screens, dials and instrument banks stacked behind me. When I looked down at myself to see if I still had my arms and legs, all I could see were tubes connected to every part of my body. Needles were stuck into my skin in what seemed to me to be every available bit of space.

As I became more aware of what was going on, I found that I had made the front page of newspapers all over the

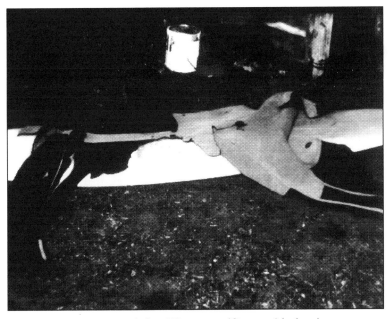

Bite out of the Wetsuit. *(Steve Absher)*

northwest. No one had ever survived so savage an attack by a Great White Shark. I was also told that the doctors held a press conference. Television crews came in from Portland and Seattle. Other crews headed out over the ocean at Cannon Beach, hoping to spice up their stories with sightings of the shark.

Terry Link, the local fish and wildlife expert from Astoria, Oregon, arrived in Cannon Beach to examine the jaw print in the surfboard. He needed to find teeth or fragments of a tooth to make a positive identification of the type of shark that had attacked me. He was unable to find even one fragment on the surface, so he had the board taken to Oregon State University to be radiographed. Through that method, they were able to discover one small tooth fragment a quarter of an inch long. From that they were able to make a positive identification that it had been a Great White, whose scientific name is Carcharodon Carcharias.

The remainder of the day I lay in my bed, so heavily sedated I did not realize where I was or even that I was alive. By the second day excellent care had stabilized my condition. However, every time the morphine wore off, the pain would again tear through my body. I'd never hurt so badly in my life. Sharp pains stabbed into every portion of my legs, arms, fingers, toes, back, chest, stomach—you name it!

When I started to moan and groan and twist about in the bed, nurses, who seldom left my side, injected morphine into the I.V. which was inserted into a vein in my arm. When the morphine entered my blood stream, it was such a wonderful relief from the pain. My eyes would roll back and I would drift off into space. They kept me heavily sedated through the second day, although, by the end of that day, I had begun to become aware of things going on around me and of my body.

Dr. Ahmad stopped by my bed during his evening rounds, holding my arm while he explained that I had survived an attack by a shark. He read the fear in my mind as my eyes focused on the many dials and screens connected to my body with tubes and wires. He carefully explained the use of each. Then I again drifted off into sleep, not remembering what he said, or much else about those first two days in cardiac recovery.

It sure made me realize how easily a person could get hooked on drugs. The sedation kept me floating in a wonderful but illusory world of no worries, pain or apprehension.

By the third day I surprised the medical staff with the remarkable recovery I had been making. They unstrapped me and allowed me to sit up in bed. My ex-wife and friends were allowed to visit. The doctors let me watch television. I seem to recall it was a football game. However, what really happened that third day is still a bit vague, because a couple of different times I was given shots of morphine to control the pain.

Later that night I awoke to find myself alone. I did not know where I was or what had happened. I was not even sure who I was. I was sweating so badly, that my bed and covers were soaked. I was so scared I began to shake. It was most likely from coming down off the morphine. When a nurse came in to check on me, I grabbed her and held her close, to make sure I was still alive. I had to hold on to something real. After that, I was given less and less morphine.

On the morning of the fourth day, they removed all tubes and wires from my body. For the first time since the attack, I was free to move my arms and legs. I was just getting used to my new freedom of movement when a nurse stopped by my bed to tell me about a four-year-old boy, also in cardiac recovery, who had just had open-heart surgery and was lonely and scared. His bed was only a few down from mine and she thought maybe if I talked with him, I could cheer him up.

It felt good to be able to do something for someone else. I pushed myself up to a sitting position, then got to my feet. I picked up a surfing magazine one of my buddies had left me and walked the short distance over to his bed.

He seemed to pep up when I sat down on the side of his bed and went through the magazine, showing him photos of guys surfing big waves. His eyes got really wide as I described my experience to him. I lifted my gown to show him the stitched scars running the length of my back. I was amazed at how well he was taking his own operation. I had to fight back tears when he asked me if I was going to be all right. A nurse stopped by later and thanked me for cheering him up.

Later that day, Dr. Ahmad looked in on me again and said I was recovering very well and that I was to be moved from cardiac recovery to another room the following morning. I sort of hated to leave the recovery ward. I had certainly received special treatment.

Recovery in the Hospital

The next morning I was placed in a wheelchair and moved to a private room on the seventh floor. The hospital's public relations official stopped by to tell me that every television news channel and newspaper in the state wanted to interview me. Dr. Ahmad said that it would be all right, but he wanted me to rest for a couple more days so that I could get my thoughts together before facing reporters. Only my close friends were allowed to visit.

The hospital photographer came by to visit and give me some pictures he had taken during the operation. He went over each photo, describing what had happened and what was done by the surgical team. I was shocked, totally unable to believe that what I was seeing were pictures of myself. That same day a friend brought me a book about sharks. I had always known about sharks and worried about them to some extent while surfing, but with the book, I really began to learn about them.

An elementary teacher from a nearby kindergarten class came by to give me 18-by-12-inch get-well cards her students had drawn for me. I still treasure each of the many get-well cards I received while I was in the hospital and I received literally dozens. I did not know there were so many wonderful caring people.

On the third day after I moved to my new room, reporters began to drop by to interview me for the local television news channels. The media people were actually lined up outside my door and down the hallway. Only one reporter was allowed into my room at a time.

In addition to the reporters who came to my room, I got phone calls from all over the country. The National Enquirer sent a beautiful lady all the way to Oregon from the east coast to write a story about me. She stayed around for several days and treated me with special kindness. It was great!

I recall one of the days I was all alone, lying on the bed looking through the photos of my wounds which were taken during the surgery. That's when the reality of it all really hit me hard. I had come so close to death and I could not deny the mental trauma the attack had caused. The next thing I knew I was crying uncontrollably.

From then on, every day there was someone who wanted to do a story about the attack and my recovery. If I didn't feel up to it the nurses would turn them away, telling them to come back later when I felt better. I don't think anybody ever was treated better than me. I really felt such concern and real caring from all the hospital staff.

A day or so later a doctor came in to remove my stitches. He had me lie on my stomach, then started snipping and pulling out the stitches that had held me together. I had a strange sensation when I turned my head to watch him pull the thread from my back. I must admit, it worried me that I might open up again if I moved.

Dr. Ahmad told me I should exercise my left arm as soon as possible. At first it not only worried me to move it too much, but it hurt. However, I did as I was told, lifting it, then holding it straight out from my body. I would walk up and down the hallway, lifting, then stretching my left arm. Most people, including the nurses and some of the doctors could not believe I was already up and walking about.

Each day they cut down on the pain medication. Whatever they replaced the morphine with did not work as well. The pain began to set in with a dull throbbing sensation invading my body. I also had a stinging sensation in the tips of my fingers and toes. According to the doctors, this was caused by the major nerve damage I had suffered. The sorest spot on my back was where the shark's teeth had scraped off layers of skin leaving it open and raw.

I was really surprised when Dr. Starr came to my room to inform me that I was to be released from the hospital the next morning. He attributed my remarkable recovery to my having been in such good shape from doing physical labor and from surfing. I didn't really want to leave. I had never been treated better in my life.

Since I did not have any clothes when I was admitted, Steve's girlfriend and his sister brought me new socks, tennis shoes, a sweat suit and a stocking cap with a "superman" sign on it.

My friend Potts, who lived in Portland, came by on the day of my release to take me to his home. Potts and I grew up together in Houston, Texas and were good friends.

I had spent a total of 11 days in the hospital. Although I was happy to be alive, I was scared to face life on the outside, knowing it would be very different than what I was used to.

As the nurse wheeled me to the exit, my friends surrounded me. One was carrying my surfboard, another the get-well cards and gifts people had given me. I realized as I went through the door and onto the street, that my time of being treated like royalty had come to an end. Gritting my teeth, I stood up, took my surfboard under my arm, and walked to the waiting car. It was then, again, that cold reality slapped me hard across the face. I realized I had been badly chewed up and spit out and I'd nearly lost my life!

 # Chapter XI

BACK TO SURFING

The fifteen to twenty seconds in the jaws of that Great White Shark seemed to be to me infinitely longer than the time since the attack.

People and friends tell me there must be a reason for me to be alive. Other than the prompt, excellent care I received by my surfing buddies, the paramedics and the doctors from two hospitals, I can think of none. Maybe the reason was for me to write the book about the true-to-life nightmare that is still very vivid in my memory to this day.

I am glad it has taken so long to put the story together. Many recollections still flash through my mind — things about the attack, the harrowing hours on the way to the hospital and the painful weeks of recovery, both physical and mental. The years have allowed me to put both the attack and my life into a perspective.

Although my sons, Jeremy, four and Justin, three, were constantly on my mind, I did not get to see them until several weeks after the attack. On that fateful day, they had been with my ex-wife, Sherri, as they drove along the north fork of the Smith River outside Reedsport, Oregon. When the announcement came over the radio that a surfer from Reedsport had been attacked by a shark and was in critical condition, Sherri knew immediately it was me. There weren't any Cannon Beach surfers from Reedsport.

Shocked, she slowed the car, then as tears blinded her eyes, she pulled off the road. The boys became worried when their mother began crying. She tried to explain to them that the person who had been attacked by the shark may have been their father.

Once she regained control, she drove to her parents' farm back down the river, only to have her fears confirmed. The hospital had phoned there to get permission from her or her parents to operate.

The boys were still too young to fully understand what had happened, but not too young to ask questions. "Is Daddy going to die? Did the shark bite his arm off? When can we see him?"

Leaving the boys with her parents, Sherri drove to the hospital in Portland to see me. By the time she arrived, I was out of surgery but under heavy sedation and still too groggy to know much of what was going on.

At home the boys kept hearing flashes over the radio about the attack and my being near death. According to their grandmother, each time they heard the announcement, they became quiet, realizing something terrible had happened to their father.

Back to Surfing

It was a wonderful experience when I did get to see them, although they seemed surprised that I still had two arms and two legs! Of course they had to see and feel the scars. As I felt their little hands gently touching my back, it really hit me how wonderful it was to be alive, to be able to be with them again.

The next day after my release, Potts and I went steelhead fishing up the coast at The Claskanie River. I shared with him on the way that I was happy to be alive, but also I was worried that I would never surf again, or even be able to work again. When we arrived, to get to the fishing spot we had to cross the river, then climb an 100-foot embankment before walking up a trail to the fishing holes. I quickly became exhausted and told him to go ahead while I rested. By the time I joined him, he had a steelhead on the line. Handing me the pole he told me to reel it in. I fought the fish for ten minutes, but lost it. Stiff, sore muscles and tight bandages around my chest made me feel like a statue, barely able to do anything except to rigidly hold the rod.

At the end of the day, I had Potts drop me at my buddy Steve's house. Steve had been in the water with me the day I was attacked. I then remained with Steve through the Christmas holidays.

Locals at Cannon Beach and many surfers from the surrounding areas organized a "shark fund" fundraiser. Because I could not work and had no money, the money they raised helped me through a very trying time. Surfing Magazine had another "shark fund", that raised money to help pay my hospital bills. People all over the world wrote letters and sent money to Seaside Hospital. The local surfers obtained a top surf movie,"Going Surfing" by Bud Browne, and donated the money they collected. Surfers and others came from hundreds of miles up and down the coast to watch the movie. It was unreal! I had never been treated so wonderfully in my life.

As the days passed I gained strength, which allowed me to walk along the beach and to watch guys surf. It was cold and rainy, forcing me to wear heavy rain gear, but the surf was very good. It depressed me to watch surfers rip the waves while I stood depressed and discouraged on the rocks.

I was further depressed by wondering what would become of my life, whether I would ever be able to return to carpentry, to even be able to support myself. The doctors were amazed that I was alive. So was I. Finally I pulled myself together and decided I was going to get back in shape.

Mark, a friend in Portland, invited me to stay with him. Every other day I exercised, walking, running, and doing a lot of pushups and isometrics. That went on for about six weeks before I began to feel confident in myself. On the inside, I was still afraid, worried that I might never be able to surf again. At any rate, it was time for me to get back to the coast and get on with my life. Two and a half months had passed since the attack, and I wanted very badly to surf again. I had to discover if I could get the ever-present fear of the ocean and sharks out of my system.

Steve once again invited me to his house to stay with him. The next day was the day I had thought so much about. I was determined to get back into the water, but I didn't have a wetsuit or a board, so Steve let me use his. We walked down the cobblestone point. We didn't talk much, even though it was a long walk. I was determined not to let the fear buried deep inside me control my life.

The surf was six to eight feet, which was probably too big for my first session, but the size of the waves made it more challenging. I approached the water's edge hesitantly. I slowly eased my board into the chilly water. It felt both wonderful and terrifying to be back in the ocean once again. The waves really were big and I felt them beckoning to me. The fear was there— pounding in my chest, but so was that undeniable love for the waves and the challenge of looking for that perfect ride! I slid

First time out after the attack. *(Steve Absher)*

onto my board and paddled toward the break. I was able to catch five waves, shaky on every one of them, but surfing nonetheless. There was a large sea lion swimming around, which made me nervous. Suddenly, I felt the urge to get out of the water, to get back to shore. After my last wave, I paddled into the shallows and very carefully walked over the slippery rocks. However, when I reached a flat rock, I turned and looked out at the ocean and knew I was cured. I raised my hands and thanked the Lord that my fear was under control. I could still surf. The feeling of internal peace was awesome.

The next week I was back at work. Jack and I rented a house at the ocean and life got better. All I wanted to do was surf, surf, and surf. I actually felt I had to, if I was to keep the fear of sharks from taking hold again.

EPILOGUE

Isnapped out of the trance I was in and finished the beer I was drinking. I grabbed my board and paddled out to where R.T. sat in the line up waiting for a wave.

With each paddling stroke, I imagined a dorsal fin out of the corner of my eye on the choppy texture of the ocean

Me surfing in Hawaii. *(Leroy Metsker)*

Great White-crusing. *(Howard Hall-H.H.P.)*

surface. I also knew that the shark that got me was still lurking somewhere, hopefully several thousand miles away.

My thanks continually go out to all those who helped me recover from the most traumatic experience of my life, those who contributed to my well being and those who prayed for me. To me, you really helped to make this world a wonderful place to live. These days when I surf the beautiful waters of Hawaii, it is with the respect of the ocean and a deep sense of thankfulness and gratefulness to be alive. I thank God for having a hand on my shoulder.

Kenny Doudt